does this
make me
a witch?

does this make me a witch?

A POETRY COLLECTION

NICOLE JENNIFER MILBURN

Charleston, SC

www.PalmettoPublishing.com

does this make me a witch?

First Edition

ISBN: 978-1-68515-790-6

Prologue

"And then I looked to my daughter, her ears almost looked tilted with interest, her inquisition high, her eyes sparkled with delight, the unknowing of the state of our world made practice all that we could do...and so I asked her with a voice rich in majesty, eyes light and whimsical, lips not sparing or lacking confidence..."do you want to see me do magic?"

Concrete Stairwell

I wonder what a parent must think of, if not their children when they're dying, sinking into what could seem like nothingness. When all of the chances that they had or wanted to have are over. The concrete stairwell...gosh, what else could you think of, if not children, that only had you left.

And I always told my father not to worry about me. But I wonder, in his last moments on this earth, if he worried for me, could there even exist a capacity for that?

I wonder if he worried knowing my brother couldn't fill his shoes...or worried knowing I'd become what I am. An unorthodox flourishing mind wanting to live a lot more each day, a mind with beauty as its armor. The beautiful armor of a fragile woman, a woman raised by a man. So, a woman with outer strength of optimism, yet inner surrender of a woman not knowing a mother, not knowing nurture.

Did he worry knowing that most of my tears would originate from happiness, not knowing that such a thing could belong to me...that I'd be obsessive, having a deep appreciation for life that I'd hold secret, cherishing moments that most take for granted, holding them forever in my mind, a fear of that contentment never returning, and that all resulting in exhaustion.

I wonder if he worried for me knowing that I'd be a soul that only one could ever understand, and the traveling I'd have to do to find them, or maybe he would have worried knowing the subconscious level of my expressed womanhood would be trimmed with ecstasy, driving men wild without them being the soul of comprehension...leaving me with a trail of men, enticed by the beautiful armor and the way it moves...nothing more, nothing less.

He had to worry for me, he saw what I'd become, he had the gift...so he left me with seedlings and barely started canvas paintings, a medley of images and words all a part of his genius.

I wonder if he worried for me knowing I'd be a woman of intense inquisition, irrational spontaneity, with a daily growing intellect, a spirit not quite equipped for this world with deranged leadership skills that would push away most of the people I know.

Yeah...of course he worried for me, my worst fear, even as a child, had always been loneliness, and he knew that...that loneliness started before the concrete stairs...

Hear Me

Please tell me you're ready to hear my story. Tell me you have endless time, while we lay under moonlight...that you'll silence the world, only you and nature a witness to my memoir. An era of sound filtered just for my words and the soft sound of maneuvering water in a nearby lake.

Tell me you can put an end to my disoriented timeline...that you have the cure for my urgent need to write more than I speak.

A Song

He asked me why I write poetry, I told him no one listens when I speak and I need a place for my thoughts.

He said I have a beautiful voice, that maybe I should start singing, perhaps that will get their attention.

So I sang to him.

Europe

I may have been here before. I say "here", meaning Europe. Stone stairs wrapped in stone walls frighten me, memories of the colosseum. I took my death here.

Possibly after an evening of performance antics, center floored in the quarters full of the Kingsmen. Music speaks to me that way, the performance pressure, the mandatory sex drip, endless movement inviting intrusive eyes. I still need that. This bares recollection of him kissing my neck, I say "him" meaning the king. His lips spoke authoritative but softly, "no Empress of mine', his hand encased in my hair, as he led me to the stairs.

Saturday Nights

Nights like these I need you. When my world has turned black and my feelings make no sense, you used to know that, you knew how that looked, back when you used to care. These are the times I need you, when my mind tells me to cry and I can't figure out why. I dig and search through tampered messages and misconstrued thoughts, finding no answers...that's why I need you.

On Saturday nights when all else fails, there's tip a bottle with you. Until I feel nothing, just you.

Your words become a cure, like a potion for every ailment, a spell for every memory wished away. Your words are confusing but you have to be right. We sit here on most Saturday nights, same bottle displayed, sometimes two. Every time this is forced to be my solution, we have this same conversation, every time. Every time, no results.

The Illusionist

With an embrace like that, pulling me close to you, your hands pressed too firmly against my spine.

Why do your hands fit me like that?

With you guiding me in, I almost disappear in your hollowness. How do you do that? How can you feel that way?

My body enclosed in you as you proceed to wrap me in your cocoon.

Perhaps this is what I've been yearning for, extreme closeness. Or perhaps this is why you hurt so bad, there's nothing inside you.

Secret

Being in love alone is like having one of the biggest secrets in the world.

It's like riding a rollercoaster with no hills.

It's like walking on a beautiful path, a garden filled path, only with no destination.

It's like driving a road, a long winding road, a meandering road, with no feeling of the motion.

Like dancing a beautiful dance that never slows to a kiss.

You know, it's like reading a one-thousand-page fairytale that has the wrong ending.

It's wasting a perfectly good glass of 1787 Chateau Lafite because it has his name on it and he has no idea.

Maybe I'll tell him there's a glass of wine here, with his name on it.

Fallen Leaves

He wasn't done yet, so he lied again. Leaves fell gracefully from trees that didn't fret the loss for they knew the return would be better than the latter. The entire setting seemed inappropriate. I wanted there to be peace here instead there was friction. The air felt like rain but of course it wouldn't, that would make me too comfortable.

The bench we should be sitting on is eons away and so are you, or so it feels. My ears are sort of ringing, but there is also a train nearby. Air keeps leaving my lungs hurriedly without me exhaling.

When I transitioned to natural brows, I didn't know you hated it, you never said anything. And when natural brows became natural everything, you still didn't say anything. You used to look at me inside and out, not up and down, what is this?! Please get to the point, I don't want to still be standing here when this train comes.

And then I wondered, as your lips continued to move in slow motion, and you tried to tell me you were going back to "what's her name", I wondered what it would feel like to be hit by a ton of bricks because I think that's what this is. Then I thought, fuck the bricks, there's actually a train close by and you said this wouldn't happen again.

Leaves fell to more leaves and there still wasn't any rain. It also felt like there wasn't any you just a whole lot of her. It felt like my legs broke at my knees but I was still standing. It felt like the air traveled with you as you turned to walk away. It felt like, I needed rain to happen just so something else would happen.

I wanted to drop to my knees and do the fetal position thing, crying all over myself, all over the grass, all over our memories, all over the fact that my period is late, all over our plans to live in Venice, all over you telling me I shouldn't have abandonment issues, all over the last three years, all over I'm fucking alone again...only my body wouldn't let me move. Instead, I stood there, like the Bristlecone Tree, dry faced, with a brain full of misfire. I worked hard at remembering all the things I've learned, all the things that weren't wrapped in images of you. And I kept standing there, in our park, sort of close to our bench, in the grass, very close to the fallen leaves. Staring into the space that once held you is where I looked for comfort until I felt the rain. Leaves fell and the rain fell but I didn't. Instead, I decided your decision wasn't for me to take personally. And the rain fell so heavily that it gave me the chance to hear my own voice repeating the words,

"it's impossible for the tracks of that train to be my destination if my legs just broke at my knees and I'm still standing."

When you have to force yourself to fall out of love with someone, respect leaves with the love.

A Child Taken

I have taken a child.

I have taken a child through its birth canal. I have given that same child my body, willingly and unwillingly. I have given this child my tears, brought them through fears. Mid nights creating images tiny minds can't piece like the puzzles taught. I have given instruction, knees follow hands, one foot in front of the other. I have given this child my bow, my knees, back to childhood, a playful imagination born of tiny things overlooked. I have taken this child from wet diapers to potty time, no watch. I have given confidence in curls! I have reincarnated energy during the crash, sleeping with one eye open due to your innocence. I have given cuddles with smiles when weeks, even months were going south. I have given cures and remedies wee hours of the night, your foot against my leg my thermometer.

I have anticipated your hand embrace, even though my step has a great pep. I have given courage through first day jitters. I have answered questions about the boy in class who always looks sleepy. I've answered questions I don't have answers to, "Hey Siri". And others we created our own answers, for they had never been written.

I have soothed through endless tears when realization hit that one day, I will become your ancestor. I have instilled in this child that sometimes mommies and daddies don't stay in strong love forever. I have given weekends and wrapped work schedules around time I'd rather spend with you. We, Netflix and chill.

I have loved beyond my fathomable capabilities of love. I have given a child ALL of my world. My life before her I was preparing for her, my life after her is to prepare her for her.

Is there A Point

We live in a world where women don't listen to their instincts until Maury tells them to.

We live in a world where you're told what the truth is, before you can find it on your own.

We live, in a world, where young minds are exposed to musical lyrics that destroy the meaning of sex.

A world where...

We encourage young GIRLS to stop their bodies from working, suffocation of ovaries, so their sex can be casual.

We live in a world where the mind can't do what it wants, only what it's taught.

We live in a world masked, in a world programmed.

And not enough people wonder why. Not enough wonder "what's the point?

If enough of us wondered what the point was...

I bet we'd make a new one...

Guidance Team

My father didn't give me everything I wanted. He made sure I had what I needed, more importantly he fed my soul. My father gave me respect, unconditional love and care beyond his own. So that's what I know, that's how I move.

This is the impact we have on our children. What we give them is what they will give to the world.

We have to be mentally sound, emotionally well for our children. By the time they need to process their own stress we can't be so burdened with our own that they fend for themselves. Parental guidance is to never stop.

Tiny Hands

She played with my curls today, while I lay in her lap for a change. Her fingertips so small, toiled in curls that laced the nape of my neck where sweet sensitivity lives.

Her focus moved to the necklace that lay resting atop of my scar, only her interest, not in that which was shiny...she examined the side of my neck with slow gentle fingers, feeling gingerly over the keloid skin of my eighteen-year-old scar as if it still felt pain. I wondered what she thinks of me.

I wonder if she feels the presence of profoundness with every touch. I wonder if she's happy we're a team. She's the little girl with all the answers, most times, not needing mine.

I wonder what she thinks of my answers to all of her whimsical questions, my matching unorthodox responses. My barbaric beliefs in what life should be and how it should be swam, fully submerged in a world we truly know nothing about, only that we must survive. Fed by the words of a being that knows nothing for you but obsequious love...a love built with plenty of smiles celebrating success.

I wonder if she is thankful for me, while we kind of wing it. I wonder what she might tell people when I'm gone.

Moon Crush

My mom once told me, whenever you miss me at night and the moon is in view, just watch it, and know that I am watching it too.

That was her way of teaching me she was close despite her absence. I wonder who taught her that. I wonder if that has anything to do with why I occasionally crush on the fullness of the moon. Or maybe it's my love of everything untouched by man that my father instilled in me. I wonder how many nights she looked at the moon through hazy, distorted vision. I wonder how many times the moon danced for her. I wonder if she ever looked at the moon and thought about how much I might have needed her.

Dear Moon Crush, Dear Mommy,

On this very night for whatever reason, I can picture it like I never have in memory. I can picture the sheets of loose-leaf paper cut mid page, stapled sloppily along the left-hand side. My homemade book titled, "Letters to Mommy". I wrote that one letter to you when I learned your departure meant a never return. The night that I clutched my eleven-year-old face, with heartbreaking questions of why I never got to see you and why I won't ever again. On this night, I think I missed you. I missed the thought of sharing a moon glance with you. I missed that I looked nothing like you, and I think I wanted to tell you that in the biggest number I could imagine. Those zeros ran right off the page, as I tried to write whatever infinity-thousand looked like. That was all I ever wrote to you, that was all I ever knew about you.

With Love and Courage

Be present, don't allow so much of your time to feel wasted.

You can't touch everyone, have some standards, be aware of your energy sharing.

ADVANCING YOUR CONSCIOUSNESS has become a survival skill.

If you're not feeling pleasant, work it out in your own space, don't project it on other people.

Remember that most problems have simple solutions; anger only holds things up.

Vibrate higher, breathe deeper, hug longer.

In the Wind

What if the wind was stealing thoughts from me?

Very much like it takes unwelcome energies.

If it does nothing for me, then why does it exist?

Why is it strong when my emotions are, carrying them to further heights? My mind planting seeds of great passion, to then be carried off to a place where they matter, in some other world equipped with sophisticated understanding.

If this wind is doing nothing for me, then why am I controlling it?

Woman

That woman that no man really wants to get to know because she's so pretty. When she walks, she becomes unknowingly sexy. It's startling, yet subtle, its effortless. Most people can't stand it and she has no idea. Women wonder, what's the occasion for such a "put on" stride.

Men wonder...how she moves in bed or how that movement would look in his private quarters. Better yet, how she looks stripped down, wearing nothing but her wildly dancing curls as they bounce to her beat of seduction. He wonders, how fast she would give it up. He wonders how tight it is and how hard he can pull her hair while he treats his body like a shovel in hers. He wonders what she sounds like under physical, sexual pressure. He wonders how many times he can maneuver and manipulate her and if her body will react. He wonders whether or not she likes the taste of sex...come to think of it, she does have nice lips. This is the excitement of the man, as he tries to determine if he could go raw or not.

But what happened to the woman?

What happened to her striking beauty and wanting to sit with her? Wanting to sit with her, looking into her beautiful eyes, while falling in love with the tone of her voice. What happened to understanding her and getting to know her? Perhaps she's funny, a great cook, an even better mom. Maybe she doesn't come from a huge family and one of her goals is to change that. Maybe she's into sports, even video games, maybe she loves to dance, is a fantastic singer and loves music of all styles. Maybe she's poetic! Maybe she loves to laugh and knows how to make all situations better with optimism. Maybe she comes equipped with the perfect plan to defy societies breeding of unsuccessful couples. Maybe, she's even more sexy than the fantasies portray, to that deserving man of course. The man willing, to simply, hear her story.

Red Lips

I hope I haven't ruined anything by crawling into your new born crevice of love. But to be honest, I hope my dream compatible image equipped with a soundtrack of moaning crescendo appears in your mind from time to time. I hope you miss me as much as you can visualize me.

Visions so vivid that you feel the tips of my fingers digging magnetically into your skin.

And you feel my struggling breathes as multiple orgasms try to suffocate me.

And the curls that tickle your pelvic bone in slow motion as you watch from above, these red lips.

I hope I appear in your mind from time to time, that was my goal.

Smudged

Sorry my lipstick is smudged, I thought you'd find it sexy; the crazy hair matches as well as the torn stockings. I'll leave my pumps on, I know you like that. And really, I just came here to dance for you.

I want to show you what Yonce meant when she wasn't sure why she couldn't keep her fingers off it. Moving my body slow to a song of your choice while I pretend my hands are yours. I'll spin for you saving the serious stuff for when I'm closer to you, more like on you.

When you can't take it anymore, I want to play, make sure you keep score.

Use this, while I create a trail that'll start with a kiss, I promise I can handle it.

Horsepower

She never really had a chance, his force was too unbearable, not that he was fast, just far more powerful than anything measured by horses.

His grasp unshaken. His body temperature too warm. The air he breathed existed to close to her lips. His tone, one of influence, the richness and darkness driven by demand. Though his words never spoke of how much he loved her, his palms did, as he held her body close, as if this ride was the one into eternity. His lips spoke wordless, for his mouth, it never stopped. His touch intrusive, uncomfortably penetrating, nonetheless, it's never enough to forfeit. With hands climbing her collarbone, aggression forces her to share words she wants to keep. His scent remains as one of pheromones alone, this is the only thing calming about him, it helps when her breathe lacking voice quivers, "okay, I love you".

Be unforgettable,

be haunting.

Far Away

I need a cabin far, far away, without you. I need a pen dipped in ink whilst a feather sits atop, without you. I need to sit alone finding thoughts, without you.

I need thoughts not grown of you; ideas not summoned by the mere thought of touching you. I need not to have blinks of motionless time just to see a clearer image of you as I watch my heart spill all over you. I need not wallow in the thought of eternal love with you, just to cry as my pen bleeds. I need not have a head full of fantasies that I can feel through paper yet not on my skin. I need not express superb expression with an imagination unwearied because it's carried by you, once kissed by you. I need to know I'm still a good writer, without you.

Dahling

My heart is broken again.

Even strangers can see it.

It resides in my posture and cascades on my face.

It's clear.

Like the love I've lost.

Wiping away smiles in the same stroke as runaway mascara.

His art has never been more beautiful.

To once be a part of such sincerity, that danced mortals into a state of bliss, to now, see with more parts, open eyes meeting truth.

Your secrets were more than deep.

Your dose of passion, pervading only with pain.

Incorrectly fervent.

The disguised, disconnected version of you, put that away forever in hiding.

The incognito works born with our era, paint him on.

Your art had never been more beautiful.

Mr. Forgetful

A few things you forgot to consider...

Like what my speech would become with sadness as its governor and what that does to those that wish to hear me speak.

What happens when I can't breathe through tears to explain this story of mine you promised you wouldn't obscure.

Or what happens when my mind seeks answers on a subject not perplex, and I can't focus, rolling around in pillows in a bed that used to be full of sex.

You forgot to consider what I'd move like with broken pieces, a body you once admired, I never thought your eyes could lie.

And you forgot to care what my life would become now that a fragment of it left with you.

Charm

You will never meet another woman who talks sweeter to you than I do.

You will never meet another woman that sees love the way I do, manifesting words never before spoken, whose skin attracting like mine...or whose love you can feel in your dreams, attached souls that entwine when our bodies can't.

You will never meet another woman whose design is true love, not the love immaturity speaks of. It's a love so deeply rooted that it pulls at her every being, deep beneath her, where she cannot see it, she can only feel it. She can only dispense it, even in not knowing it.

You will never meet a woman truer, who will see you close to the way I do. A woman whose purpose will be you, whose journey will be born of you, whose admiration of you will hold purpose forever. A woman who will remember your every word, understanding that when you speak it's for a reason.

You will never meet another woman whose love feels, moves, speaks or lasts quite the way mine does. Another womans love will never suffice...even if she does happen to be another poet.

Starry Eyes

My story won't have a cliffhanger at the end of every episode but it will leave your starry eyes full of tears wondering, how I keep surviving.

I Promise

I'm sorry I cried like my world was over when I knew you were coming.

I'm sorry I stopped having all the answers as your questions grew in intelligence. I'm sorry you've witnessed tears.

I'm sorry it's just you and I.

I'm sorry, because I promise, my life began when you finally came. I'm sorry, because it didn't matter, now we answer seek together. I'm sorry but real mommies cry too. I promise you; life happens the way it's supposed to, and I'm in love with it as you and I.

Your Highness

When you know how to wrap your love up, no frills left undone. When chapters are ended, so are the books. Removal of Your Highness when reciprocation is unmindful, inexperienced, unaware.

Your seriousness, controlled by extreme seriousness. Being one with your feelings, the only people you miss, are your ancestors.

Certified Nutcase

The voice spoke again as she stood before the mirror.

"Look at you, you know what you're doing, you know why they talk to you that way", he chuckled...a chuckle that seemed to roar against the windows with an echo all its own.

"Just look, look at the way you trace your own skin, the way your gaze, ever so sensual, traveling slow, from curve to curve, peak to peak, you stand mesmerized as you dance in your own arms. The appearance of your skin, caressed by fingertips of red excites your senses, a bit more than it does the man...I wonder why?" The voice continued, as did she.

"Can you even hear me?"

On Paper

My body manifests this over and over.

I'm not sure why, I mean, I'm sure why, I just I can't make it look good in paper.

It's a perpetual representation of me, that I

wish looked good on paper.

As your wondering, "What is she talking about?"

I'm practicing my handwriting.

Not a Nightmare

Last night you came to me in my dream and that was almost enough. I can feel it when you're not here and that makes staying asleep harder. I can't tell if I'm supposed to be an amazing lover here or a beautiful poet here. I don't know if I'm meant to fall in love or if I'm meant to help everyone else fall in love.

The Audacity

What have you accomplished?

Someone just asked me, in a malicious manner, what have I accomplished in life.

At first thought the question thumped hard in my diaphragm with heaviness that heated my insides, it took my breath away...I didn't know how to answer. I didn't own a house, nor do I own expensive things. The credentials behind my name are mediocre at best. I have nothing to present to any of you to boast, "Look, I'm important and accomplished, these are my things".

But what I do have is a learning, advancing consciousness. I am a woman that learns from my mistakes. I don't take many chances because they don't always make sense to me. I don't love hard, I love appropriately. I know what true dedication is and I know far too well what it means to heal friends and strangers alike. I understand what it is to level up from immaturity. I know what it feels like to live in uncertainty without goals. I know what's it's like to live in certainty with goals of eternity. I know what it feels like to walk away. I haven't yet learned why the heart breaks and catches fire, but I know how it feels and how it heals. I understand what it means to truly forgive, I didn't always. I learn from others, whether the experience negative or positive. I know how to listen. I know my energy. My mind can quiet, I know how to be present. I'm a survivor...with a protégé. My days have highlights. Any frustration can be suppressed. Anger doesn't live with me. I understand that sometimes the reason things happen isn't important and that what's important is that it did happen, and then there's the space where it's no longer happening, it's no longer active, and that's your time to reflect and move through it. I have the courage to put others first. I have profound empathy. I know how to love a stranger with all of me, I understand how to wrap their world into mine because the universe spoke of motherhood. I know selflessness.

I can offer creation, in a true human experience. I'm a writer, a mother, a daughter, a thinker, I question things without allowing the unknown to determine bliss or not...I am a mirror of my true existence, I am happy. No man defines me, nor do I require sex to feel higher. I see through the unnecessary and effortlessly avoid. I treat life as an adventure, not to be mistaken with routine. My goals are set around experiences and consciousness, I have no interest in collections.

So no, if you want a space of things I have invested in or purchased, I am here to tell you that I will disappoint...but standing here alone, I can teach you a lot. When should we start your healing?

Today I spotted the bird that was leading the flock. Alignment.

My Thoughts

It says type your thoughts here, well my thoughts are off limits right now. What it should say is, type your thoughts here that are share friendly and non-offensive...or type thoughts here that won't allow anyone to know your deepest secrets.

It should say, share with us here how miserable your day was, tell us how you spent your entire day in reflection of what's really going on. Tell us how on your down days no one is there for you. Write about how you can't seem to understand why your worst fear is to be alone, yet so many times, you're all alone. Write about how you live in and out of sadness as much as you fight it because you have a job to do. Tell us about the truth and how you cry so beautifully, yet no one is ever around to witness it. Talk about how sensitive you are, how sometimes deciphering emotions is the hardest thing in the world.

Share with us again, how hard it is to be a woman...and how under-fucking-appreciated we are.

Karma

How long are you allowed to blame someone's bad luck and inability to avoid an ill functioning life on the way they once treated you?

Until you speak to a person of profound wisdom, you will never truly know if you are wise.

Becoming Kings

What happens to the beautiful girls that don't have daddy issues. Low body counts right? Respect for all crevices for they know who is worthy of touch and who not. No need for endearing sounds escaping through moisture kissed lips, we are already convinced of our wholeness. An eye gaze with the touch of a hand instantly writes you off or signs you up, daddies make daughters magic. A no nonsense policy like the fist atop his pick. Stature like the noblest of goddesses, unbothered as the Methuselah tree.

Hugs and kisses of these women are affections that heal all, laced with genuine intentions and forever. The girls that love hard can't compare. These girls whose fathers gave life to their love, through togetherness and teachings of self-worth.

Their men, they become kings.

Of course, a lot of men want me, but

I'm gentle with myself love.

Doing the Work

When you spend a significant amount of time in your own space...healing, maturing and advancing your consciousness, you come out of that with a calculated awareness and calculated tolerance for other people. Your space is sacred. It's cleansed and protected and you treat it accordingly. You value yourself because you actively worked on your thoughts, mindset and your presence. You are functional regardless of what you see around you. Your time is precious and not warranted to many. Clarity comes regularly and you're aligned the way you're supposed to be.

I have learned that keeping this peace, is something I will fight for.

maybe passion....

maybe I'll master passion.

Little Helper

Today I had a conversation with my daughter about some things I was feeling.

Because what I was feeling was something she may experience one day. What I was feeling was heavy. I need her to understand the heaviness of emotion, I need her to understand that it can all be sorted through.

Today, I sorted through profound emotions with my daughter a witness, with my daughter my helper.

Give Me Your Secrets

You don't have to give me anything, I'll prove that. Just give me an undisguised version of yourself so I can love you for exactly who you are...with the ability to calm your nerves, knowing exactly how long it will take, by the exact touch.

I want your secrets in case they weigh you down.

Let me heal you with kisses of honesty, hands that soothe, my essence charged throughout you while we make love that our souls can feel...obsess over me, unsure how I'm your cure.

Let me stand by your side, show you the reason why you have always worked so hard, let me be the reason you know it's paying off. Allow me to be the warm body beside you at night helping you sleep, now that you're not alone. Let me help you through life's confusion, as a woman that listens with good intent. Allow me to share with you the details of this dream I had where you.............

A dream of quiet this must stay, it's the only thing that keeps me from floating away.

Fifteen Years Ago

He was the first man whose spirit touched mine. Only then, I didn't know what that was or how it felt. I was eighteen. He saw into my eyes the way no one else had. His being lived with me without hesitation, I now understand why. Our spirits connected before I was aware of spiritual connection. We shared a season, obstacles and hurdles hindered anything more. His was the first spirit to encroach on mine, and his eyes, those eyes attempted to pierce my soul but my receptiveness hadn't been born yet, that was fifteen years ago. Now your back. I don't know what to do with that.

He's come back for me, unfinished business...I can't figure out what to do with that. I felt his need for me then, and I can feel it now, it's in the start and end of his voice tone. It's in the pauses in between his words. I can feel him looking into me, even though he's ninety-five miles away...I'm not sure what to do with this. I'm pretty sure I don't belong anywhere that I'm titling "Fifteen Years Ago".

Tailored Suit

I really just wanted to be grabbed, heavy palms in my hair, face to face, tell me you'll do life with me.

Reside with me in this tiny space. In this, our space, where I can hear the inside of your chest. I can feel you here. Your energy overwhelming in this close proximity. This energy you act like doesn't exist, it pulls all over me, it pours into me.

It's when your air becomes mine that I feel like I can't breathe, you know, when we both get on at the first floor. You hold weight over me, not just the thought of hands in my hair but, you hold weight over me. This feeling, this is unmatched. This is brand new, custom tailored. You hold this weight over me, every time you come around, in your tailored suit.

Word Sorcerer

People think I start to write more when I'm in love.

I write in passion, there's a heat to it, not even this word sorcerer can produce transparency. It's a sensation that holds crown to the highest intensity...one not controlled by any familiar part of me.

Intensity so rich, so substantial it sits me down, sometimes where I stand. Thoughts that coil and uncoil as the universe has its way with me, a way I need, the origination a mystery, fueled by fierce desire, that never ever tires...an authority not ruled by me, a discovery soon to be mastered.

This is what my passion feels like, now, to figure out who I'll share it with.

From the Beginning

Nothing was going to stop this. I felt this from the beginning. I literally...felt this from the beginning. Five years ago, I think my compass was off, my sacred space, the space I was to offer him, it wasn't ripened yet. Fuck, I really felt this from the beginning...only it happened before so my radar was high, incredibly intense. I once read through eyes of lust interpreting it as eyes of sincerity. You see, my compass, it was broken. For a while, a broken compass with strong intuition was difficult to interpret. But for real, I felt this from the beginning.

I felt you. I felt the presence without seeing it as a pull on my soul, it lived deep within the pit of my root chakra waiting for me. In its wait, it didn't linger there, it may have traveled through all chakras, making a mark, signing its name, singing your name...demanding its purpose. Building a trust in us that I could benefit from instantaneously.

I hadn't met you yet, not in the flesh. This happened long ago when the timing wasn't perfect. But maybe now it is, if I could just look at you again, I would know.

Together Us

Why do you feel like everything to me? That scares me. It pushes me into a shell that I desire to live in with you. It backs me into a corner, where I back into you. In the dark, you embrace me, and I know I'm okay.

Can You Hear Me

Our souls literally communicate with each other. It's not just when you touch me, it's when you breathe on me. It's when you hover in the closest, as if to whisper in my ear, yet you say nothing. With closed eyes and escaping gasps, I can still hear you. It's when our hearts beat against one another. When we're chest to chest with a rhythmic exchange that I never want to forget. When your face touches mine I feel it in detailed time. When you taste me...I can feel it always. Our souls communicate, despite that I don't even know you...but I feel like I do. It's almost like I've had you before, exactly this way, hurting (broken) and insanely intimate. Your familiar to me and I love you for that. I don't know what comes next but having a chance at such divinity, at such connectedness, with not much else mattering, it's worth a small moment in time rather than no moment in time.

Beauty Marks

It's not a beauty mark or a skin tag, it's not even a mole, yet every time you speak to me with kissing lips close to my belly button, it seems to be your favorite spot.

Before you, a spot that went unnoticed.

But that doesn't mean anything...because if it did...

If it did...

That would mean you foresee my kisses before you taste them. That when I walk my aura sings to you, a song you remember from dreams of old. It would mean that when I look at you, with heavy thoughts, your heart quiets, for my words spoken are far more paramount than those written. It would mean that my touch belongs to you, complete with all the emotion you inadvertently desire, while your heart, forever mine.

Netherlands

You created a happiness during your era. You made me feel like you wanted me. But when I walked away you didn't stop me. You didn't come collect your things. You didn't care that I wanted to talk. You disappeared. I no longer felt wanted. But I don't think I ever was.

A Name with No Face

I think I'm supposed to break apart for you. However, you live in my spine, this will affect you too.

And lately when I think about you...I can't find your face. And you know what, last night, an angel came to me and she spoke of you. She told me why at times I think of your name, she couldn't however, make it clear why your name was the only thing I could remember. But then I remembered with us, that I wasn't looking for too much, you were just the wrong person. Again, even in creative writing, I can't think of a face for even a subtle description.

You see, poets, we have two selves. I need at least one of them to fall in love, luckily it won't be with you, you can't even get a mention. You're forgotten.

Burgundy

When I met him, he literally felt like everything I had been waiting for. He felt almost too good to be true. This felt like mine. He felt like actual love.

Then months passed us and that's when they say true colors become THE colors. Just when I was considering an abundance of love for him like he always suggested…he suddenly stopped feeling like love. And I saw colors close to those of the flags they warn of. He felt to me like someone that maybe pretended in love. He began to feel like a man that was about something much different than what I could ever desire. So my heart started to crumble a bit…and just as I was trying to give the strongest part of myself to him…the promised disappointment hit, aggressively, again. I became the unseen, unloved and unappreciated. Used.

So my heart broke right there in my hand as I attempted to give it to him. I held onto it like that for a while, for too long I think, in a state of panic, not meditation.

I never knew how a broken heart would materialize until I had to gaze upon mine…a heart dismantled, almost dissected from failed suspension of the bountiful cord promised to be safe. I had never seen myself this way, saturated in devastation that I prayed wasn't my own stupidity. Holding tightly to a heart I had only ever felt but never seen, until now...it saddened something else inside me to witness the defeat.

And eventually when the bleeding stopped, a search for this demolished heart, nearly abandoned...it sat alone in a mirage of all the shades of burgundy. This sight more daunting than before. Cleaning ensued for days, even weeks - only to find that it was still broken, truly dismantled...one of its parts to never return. For reasons unspoken, this broken heart will forever be the one I'm still struggling to fit back into my chest.

Sometimes you have to apologize to yourself...then do better...again.

Yours

The thing you feel outside of religion that's your spirituality.

The thing that you feel outside of doctrines, outside of the proposed, outside of the suggested...those things not alongside prerequisite designs and structures...the thing that you feel without being told what to feel...

that's your spirituality.

Flat Earth

I experienced so much loss.

Then the loss stopped, but I think that's what I became used to.

So, I held the tightest to what I did have. My consciousness started to elevate, that must have been a thank you.

Then I wanted to fall in love.

But I couldn't, I thought I was broken inside.

There was something I didn't understand here. I may have been misinformed. Now, I'm stuck in that.

My father showed me love with no affection, it was more of that necessary love, the "I will die for you love". Now, affection is what I crave, now I require the commitment of willingness to die for me. I don't think that's too much to ask, men do exist this way. And I need to make love...like create it. Everyday... and I need to touch it. I would have to see the work.

There is also still something collapsing in my world...at the same time, something is being built. I can't identify either one. The vibrations on my skin burn in wonderment. I don't fear any of this, I know I can fix and rebuild the debris.

I'm still waiting for someone to hold me when I cry...and mean it.

And if the earth is flat...then where does it end.

Weight of the World

Have you ever looked into the eyes of a person that belongs to you? It doesn't get any heavier.

I lied.

Have you ever looked down at your legacy, your children with their children and theirs...and KNOW that somewhere in there, you did something right?

It doesn't get any heavier.

No Fork in this Road

I feel beautifully intense right now.

This is my emotional state, the connections in my brain...it's my electricity, in which I have absolute control.

I feel like divinity. I feel like...my soul vibration is high with strong intrigue. My quivering skin is continuous from every thought emanating such positivity, such radiance, such power. This alignment, lying alone, in a semi blackened room, I need to stay in this...right here, right now,

this is trust

its self-reflection

its manifestation

it's livelihood

its love

I cannot leave. I've needed this for so many years.

Still Nothing

I used to wonder what the day would bring. Turns out, it brought nothing. No turmoil, no edge, no sadness. His vibration carried no pain. I wasn't needed.

This day didn't bring any growth, reflection or realization.

Stimulation of deeper thoughts never occurred. Even in the disconnect, I waited for him to need me. An embrace of little to no energy told me, I was in fact, never needed.

Tell Me

How do you tell someone that you can erase their worst fear? When they think you don't know what they worry of at night. How do you tell someone that your life's journey, thus far, has been preparing you for them, that you've thought about it, in great detail, that it fits? When they won't know what you mean, they won't get it, or care to, it will push them away. How do you tell someone you want every second of everyday with them? When all they will do is take it wrong. How do you tell someone you love them when you know it will make them leave you?

Soul Calls

It's the silent calls that are the loudest. The silent ones are the ones I want. They feel the absolute best. Understanding comes easy. The one sidedness begets no anxiety. The one sidedness satisfies my soul.

I thought I lost you

so I sent you one of my spirit guides

if I can't take care of you, they will.

Protected Species

I've already chosen what I'm okay healing from. I'm not taking on any new breaks, gashes or tears. Not in the business of heartbreak, I'm not designed that way anymore.

In this state of continuous healing, I'm not allowing any drama in my life and if that starts in your eyes, I'll never even speak to you.

Ever So Gently

If my spirit angel came to you...gently, would you be open?

If my spirit angel whispered to you while you slept, messages of endearment, messages of enamor, how do you think that would feel? I'd always prefer you to hear it straight from me but the timing is never right. So, if my spirit angel came to you in the night, ever so gently, please tell me you'll believe her when she tells you another angel loves you.

Time

If I could have a little more time with you

(that's all I need).

Then you would understand

(that's all I need).

Sometimes I want someone other than

myself to soothe my soul.

Then I remember, that's impossible.

2019

Vulnerable. Because inside me, my past keeps coming up. It's emotions, like, ones I already sailed through. It's feelings, like the most painful ones...from before. And all of its here, nothing is being left out. The revisits are hella painful.

It's my dreams. It's music. It's Aliyah's dad. It's my dad. It's conversations with strangers when they dig too deep. It's my relationship with my brother, our connection...someone severed it. It's that..........I am like my mom. It's that I knew her superficially and I'm like that part. It's also that she's gone. They're all gone.

It's because this moment right now, this morning...snow paves only the sidewalks, the streets are wet and black, a silver cast pulsates through the windows, glassy eyes and a throbbing head. It's my birthday weekend. I woke up alone. I needed to think about that for 1997 and 2002. I needed to go back there today, alone, in silence, in the silver cast, on my sofa.

2019, Thank you.

People have broken me and my daughter is watching. So, I decided to heal myself, endlessly, with the touch of a button.

At Thirty-three....

At thirty-three, I'm not coming out of my mind anymore. I value time too much. I value clarity and understanding.

I used to need people to know when I did something generous. Now, the only person that needs to feel that is me. I'm finally understanding that I don't REQUIRE gratitude.

I'm hoping to not take everything so 'flipping' personal...but that might have to come with the thirty-four entry.

Okay at Thirty-Three...we are actively choosing our happiness and we are showing people how that looks if they aren't there yet. We are not judging...as much. We are surrendering to all the intuitions, because they're kind of dope.

More meditation, yoga, writing, reading, aromatherapy, photography, goal planning...LESS SCREEN TIME. More healing...because that's starting to feel continuous.

More love, more cherishing the moment, more soft-spoken words, more grace, more peace...more quiet.

Cheers to hugging so much longer and vibrating so much higher.

This is a Brainstorm

This is a brainstorm. One of the lavish ones. The clouds that never before shed rain...it's sea, never before pelted on. The synapse never enticed like this, in this storm that's not a storm. This mirage of nature's mother has you to thank. The things that spiral in my beautiful places, they will project on you, more than necessary. A sorcerer's imprint with all things majestic. I will force feed you everything that my soul desires, for I know these luxuries universally. When I touch you, you'll feel how our skin needs it...every time.

I'd allow evolution with you because of how you feel, you feel like allegiance. You feel like fondness...enchantment. Your soul gentle, yet strong. It feels native to me. You feel like compassion and care. You feel like precision.

I can't be with myself to the thought of you, that's not what this is. It travels beyond, I bask in that. There isn't a person with profoundly calculated parts like yours, I'd honor that always.

If you were to speak words of endearment, they'd be born of the universe, it would have swirled between all of the worlds and then us, not to stop there. I'd never have to question it. Fears of abandonment wouldn't exist. These things, put to rest.

You bring into my world, what my father would have preferred to leave me with. This could be it. I now understand what to do with that, it creates goosebumps with intense vibrations on the skin of my chest. The goosebumps like magic. I'd love you to touch them each one by one, in slowed time controlled by you. These are my thoughts.

This is a brainstorm that I want to dance in, I want to dance to the thunder of this storm...your eyes fixated on glistening curls that drip to a waist your irrefutably in love with.

This is a brain storm I'd love to get lost in, wet, with you... living out the fantasy due to its inevitability...mirroring these thoughts, exceeding expectations. This is an aftermath I never could have predicted, you saved me...because when I didn't know I needed it you came along and you became my friend... this is a brainstorm; this is my life.

Body to Body

I want to experience my body with you. As it takes profound heights, I want it to be with you. When this body escapes reality and travels over and over again to a state of bliss I want it to be because of the heaviness of your body thrust, your hands locked into the groves of my hips, body to body with periodic hair pulling for more closeness...incredibly heated, incredibly deliberate. I want this translation to be for you. I need you to feel this. This body, this process, all with you...you will know everything you need to about my desire for you, about my love for you...about my soul, for you...

I need to get so close to you...that we cannot undo this.

Three Words

Refrain from those three words.

Instead feed me words that channel my inner poet.

Instead, smile at me in awe as I run across a field to take a picture of a dying tree.

Instead, hug me long until our bodies can't take it anymore.

Photograph me without me knowing.

Instead, let me love hard, the things I admire, assist me in the opening of my unorthodox intellect.

Stare at me as we drive down a long empty road, with the wind tearing at my hair as I smile at you, you'll never get a puzzled, "what" from me...I understand your gaze.

See my compassion and love my passion.

Seeing me unveiled will leave no room for those three words, your eyes will do the talking...and I will always understand.

If You're Ready

My heart was beating through my nightgown. It felt like the bed pulsated to its beat. My mind raced because you usually don't. What was this? The bed quakes softly and my body surged, some of you know this as vibrating, most of you know this as chills. My body became alive second after second as the thumping inside my chest grew louder. I was alone, with just thoughts of you and you inside me. Mystery for this Empath, for this Goddess, for this Aquarius Priestess...mystery, it's my kryptonite. It defeats me, it makes my heart no longer a secret. It makes my heart ring in song, for all to hear, maybe of excitement, maybe because this shouldn't happen. My senses are peaked. My vibration is misfiring and it tickles my skin. I wonder if you'll feel that way. I wonder if you'll feel like...like the allegiance I spoke of. I wonder if you are precision like I spoke of. I wonder if you'll be gentle with me. I wonder if love words will whisper between our skins, or will the voices of magic shout. I wonder if you'll remember me, I wonder if this could make you love me. I wonder if me and you, if you and I...

I wonder if this is us.

I wonder if you will allow yourself to feel like the god that you are.

Cracked

I'm 33 years old...and my life may have just cracked directly in half.

I mentioned before that I was like my mother; the extent is bothersome. I think someone showed me as a young woman how desirable I was. Now....I desire that. My life may have cracked in half but my sex didn't.

Be an emotionally intelligent woman.

Either your audience will change

or your audience will change.

Man Eater

Sometimes men come along, they speak "oh so softly" to my poet, then they leave.

And then sometimes...when water cascades over dancing hips and thighs I see the shimmer of gold.

I fall in love with myself all over again, I rinse......I repeat.

Then words pore from me with such intensity, such betrayal, that it may or may not be spun from the latest man eaten. I grovel. For no ink, no words can match the intentional pain. Intended pain found only in the deepest depths of the deepest plants through the deepest seeds. Mixed up in harmonious turmoil, you entice my poet because your mind fucks mine. The cannibalism must be stopped.

A glimpse of glitter and gold this time...I rinse...I repeat.

I went from low cut tops and

skin tight jeans to

shoulder highlighter and these beauty

marks on my lips.

Carefully Paced

That's what he liked to do. It was a skin thing. An art thing. A traced thing, carefully paced. The focus and dedication, you feel that. It was a passion thing. A passionate spiral of parted lips with matching hips. His hands were never more real. His lips, tasting for two. My body, never more alive. Rhythmic movement to insatiable breaths. Pauses in time, resets in anatomy. A continuum of blissful practice, one that actually means nothing.

It's Coming

I watched the tiniest tear fall to my thigh. It was the part of my thigh I never shaved; the hair was blonde. The tear fell into sunlight, I was okay if it stayed there forever.

I wasn't sure why my tears were awake...I felt so beautiful, skin barley clothed, my face gloating tear-soaked lashes that made mascara swell.

I wanted more tears to puddle in between my legs, only, I couldn't muster it, clarity was coming, as promised.

I blinked in slow motion on purpose, sitting there in the sun. My eyes twinkled with lashes to match, mesmerizing and wet.

I needed a hand, maybe two, not my own...ones unpredictable, one's fastidious. I needed hands...but I also needed lips, ones to speak me back to reality. Lips to trace the sun that crept on my skin.

Actually, I needed lavender pervading through the air while the smoke of sage danced in this space. I wanted to be perched high on a throne with posture fit for a queen, but right now, fetal position was all I could conjure...I sat there hugging what was left of me, I had to get through this poem.

Protected Spaces

Twice, I was in a protected space. Once it was alone, once...
it wasn't.

Walking in hand...taught me how to not. This protected space
alone...it was warm...not too warm...there was an occasion-
al cool breeze that welcomed freeness...wholeness even...the
climate encouraged oneness. The fragrance there, smelled of
sandalwood and palo santo, with a little bit of Sunday morn-
ings from the 90s.

This space was clean, it was breathable. I inhaled genuine ar-
gon there. Simple breathing invoked progress in conscious-
ness. Most of the voices were muted here...I needed that. My
thoughts were clear here, untainted, without manipulation.
You see, most of the VOICES, they were muted here. My once
familiar level of selflessness, that wasn't here with me. I didn't
miss it...I needed that. My mind belonged to me, that let me
navigate, no GPS. My body craved for nothing. Not the taste
of it nor the taste of him.

My body was whole, my soul fed, satisfied, insatiability didn't
occur here. Touch didn't happen. I touched myself. My spirit
was rich because no one lied to me. I cried only when I want-
ed to, it was beautiful. I spoke truth for I had enough time

to process what wasn't. I communicated so effectively that I never had to argue. There was no shouting, when I spoke, so did exactness. When I listened, the goal was comprehension and discovery. I was growing, in a peaceful, focused space that only I could access. This space was protected...maybe I'll go back there.

The End

So, the truth is, I felt magic to him but he doesn't want to admit it.

Then I healed him but he doesn't want to admit it.

Now I'm leaving him and he won't fucking admit it.

Sneaky Poets

Be wary of poets, for one day you may end up as carefully thought-out words etched on a page.

Thought of only once, spun on and re-mastered for their spoken word. In dim lighting, accompanied by the smell of vetiver and burning resin. A pen occasionally rests in between lips where you once did. A hand paws at tethered curls that you won't know how to forget. There's a breeze, it pulls at a nightgown you've never seen. Your remembered just that one time, through scribbled ink, you become words you'll never hear.

How to heal your hurting soul,

be good to people always from the core

of that same soul.

Dedication

One of the most hurtful things in the world is to be under attack from someone you love.

One of the most powerful things in the world is to have to hold back your spirit team.

Half Way Mark

So 2019...at the half way mark.

I've been spending a lot of time working through things on my own, not the usual bounce thoughts and ideas off of everyone around me. It feels good but it also feels bad. I don't think I give myself enough credit to make the best decisions. I'm working on that.

2019...still, has been incredibly vulnerable for me. I'm embracing that, alone, this shit builds character. It feels feisty and it feels aggressive but I need this. There's another silver-cast outside. This 2019 is something beyond what I can find words for this morning. Something is shifty here, it feels...majestic, but I'm still scared. Maybe the silver skies birth this fear, maybe it's the way my skin is fickle with vibration when I imagine living a life of mundanity; or the thought of living a man-made life.

I think I'm magic and I think I think too much. 2019 moves at hyper speed for a reason, it's my reason.

Aliyah

One day my daughter will thank me for working hard at her. For being present and engaged. We have done eleven years now and this journey brings magic every day. I can no longer pick her up, but now, I can lift her up. I can nurture her soul and plant seeds for her future harvesting. Leaving it up to her to take what she wants and leave what she doesn't. And I'm probably going to plant every seed in existence, that's what I want to be to her. See...like I said before, her soul is familiar to me, the fit is unmatched. But honestly, I'm fearful...I'm fearful because society and social media. I'm fearful because generational curses left our realm when I lost both parents before the age of 17...so the failing or fucking up is not an option, too much has been sacrificed. Being a disservice to ourselves is not an option. Not elevating spiritually is not an option.

I'm fearful because I'm working hard at this and I'm doing it alone. I value and cherish my daughters being and existence, failing her...is not an option. I see past the basis of parenting and I go beyond because she requires that. She's the best child I know and I say that completely unbiased. It's my duty to make sure she stays that way...MY STORY HAPPENED so I could LITERALLY hand write hers. I'll say it again and forever, "My life before her, I was preparing for her, my life after her is to prepare her for her".

Damn Ego

If the ego is designed to dissolve and awareness and ego cannot coexist...does that mean that people that exist in only an ego identifying nature never become aware, in turn, never truly learning who they are?

Almost There

When you can sit at home on a Friday night in a quiet room with a smile on your face because your daughter is amazing; the ultimate goal is already set; now just to evolve in this forever.

Today I told a man that I wanted to

help people for a living.

And for the first time, it didn't sound

crazy.

Not Our Bond

There's something wrong with our bond. I never felt it but the women can. It's the lingering for them. It's the, they were supposed to be connected still and it ravages at my soul every time I trip over their cord.

They feel me still existing there, more than just the child. More than just the archived footage, more than just the fact that...he still grieves the severing. His greatest adventure turned greatest feat, turned greatest mom, turned greatest... "She's actually not that bad, I should have been more kind to her."

That animosity.

They can smell tears of new still dipped in potions blended by me. They can feel the heart that thuds more controlled when I grace my presence. The subtle control that exists in the shadows of every day, both dusk and dawn. It's the intimidation, it's the inside jokes, it's the unintentional flirting, it's the read receipts. It's probably the fact that I probably come up when you attempt to face your demons. It's definitely the fact that I have risen above your demons and left unscathed. It's that you sent the demons to attack me and instead they attacked you, instead they continue to attack you. I was stronger. I won. I will always win, just like I will always love you.

See...there's something wrong with our bond.

The Line Up

When it's time to rearrange things, you have to lay them all out. You have to look at everything accurately. Sometimes the examining will cause tears, only to follow inevitable clarity. Organization might surface that feels distressing, allowing the freedom to move without obstacles.

Shifting you thought impossible will happen...that was always the goal.

Gold Digger

I'm not a gold digger baby, I like power and acquaintanceship. Small talk with strangers doesn't do it for me.

And the people I consorted with hundreds of years ago, they're all in charge now.

Veered

You want to know how I know we are completely off of our true-life path; veered from what it means to truly elevate, experience and exist?

Because people think the orgasm is the most profound thing that can happen to us.

Zoi

At first, when I miss you, I wash my entire body with my hands, no loofah. I sing a song to myself a song with no words only sounds. Water drips from my hair into my mouth, everything becomes an oral fixation, rain water does it every time. Everything smells like you, I am you...as the earth awakens, preparation for this ritual. My skin gets its oil from whatever is left from last evening and I still love the way it tastes. My body reconfigures for you even when you can't figure it, you do need me like I need you. On this evening, lonely beaded skin because your need is thin and I can't conceptualize why you're not here. I've been waiting for you in this storm and I wish the flashing didn't come from bystanders only Mother Nature.

Why are you not here? I needed this to be more clear. The songs, the dance, don't you see these crystals?! Why isn't my manifestation working? And stop telling me you still love me if you haven't even forgiven me, while these whispering voices couldn't get any louder, this air feels like smoke, my head feels like at any second it could implode. Something inside makes me feel that running the other way makes sense but my ankle feels heavy and I think these walls are concrete and I keep forgetting, I haven't touched any rain in years.

But I miss you, and I long for days when manifestation and where are my crystals? I miss when we could practice making a baby and you made me feel safe, all in the same stroke. They don't let me have my sage here and I can't find Zoi. I looked in the closets like you said and under the bed and the last thing I remember was both of us hiding and sometimes I can hear her crying but I can never get to her and I sleep with my brush because it reminds me of her rattle. I can't remember the last time I didn't feel fear. NO!

I'm not confused I know exactly what's going on and I promise, I really do promise, I'm trying this time. I'm closing my eyes again, not tight like to never open, like when I throw my head under the covers hiding from monsters that are actually there, or like the panic attacks in the middle of highways but, calm more like...like...like fluttering eyes like in meditation. I am in control.

And why is this room getting so small? I'm not losing you again, that beautiful woman with her perfect life and her perfect career and her perfect house and her perfect Instagram, the perfect mother, she cannot have you!

I need my heart to stop racing. Alright, I'm going to count to ten. 1, 2...please keep your hands off me and no I won't open my mouth I don't want your pills, your psychedelics. Sir please, you don't understand so why are you sitting so close to me? I don't like this sofa. This whole thing reminds me of that fucking movie, "Good Will Hunting". Only this is my fault, because lithium, electric shock, drowning, and poking skulls in my holes are all BULLSHIT! And give me a break! My name is not ma'am it's "Forgotten", or you can call me "Unheard" or "Swept Under the Rug".

Come on! Don't make me raise my hand...I really need to make a phone call, I need to get back to my family, I said I was sorry. They're setting me up! And they're coming, I can't be here please. Why is that lady trying to show me arts and crafts again? I'm trying to concentrate, I really need you all out of my space, you're making me feel sucked in and I don't even know what that means. I just want to be alone, wait, please. Don't leave me here by myself. Please come back, just let me hold her before you take her, I said I promise I won't hurt her. I just want to see if she looks like me. Please if you don't untie my hands, I swear I'll... Okay, okay, okay, okay I'm sorry I'll do it...99,98, 97, 96, 95, 94, 93, 92......

-In Honor of Mental Health Awareness

And never forget;

The 14th floor is the 13th floor.

Without Shade

Why do I become this way, eluding softness and sensuality. A dance with myself to a melodic portrayal...a melodic portrayal to match the beauty I hope I'm casting. A romance I'm to never share.

I could sit in a field for hours, in the sun, no hat, without shades, without shade...writing...thinking of you. I'd write by hand and it'd feel like everything I need. Nothing else would seep in, only the sun, the unpredictable breeze that paints my skin with loving whiskers...and you.

First, you'd seep in mentally; this makes my pen move. It makes me gaze into wondrous nature to pull words and phrases from mind spaces governed by such.

Next, you'd come in spiritually; it feels like finesse. It makes me surrender to spirit lead by nobility, it makes me breathe, do you know how good breathing feels? It makes me extract from myself a magic I thought limited to me being a black girl. It fills me in ways you couldn't alone.

Then physically, once I'm lying in the grass, dress and hair touching the earth, eyes closed despite the beating sun. It's only then that you will come to me physically. I'll be waiting for you...in this field, in the sun, no hat, without shades, without shade.

Ellipsis

My spirit, my intuition, my empathy...my highness...
everything that defines the woman I am, that's evolving. I'm
more open, without consenting...this sensitivity, it hits differ-
ent. Everyday filters are being removed, if not intentionally
then in error.

Usually I welcome the receptiveness, however, the resonation
is different this time. I feel everything and I can't do this alone.

Sometimes we think we know what we need...then...we don't.
When shifts happen and a new intuition ignites, your picture
changes, it absorbs differently. I literally feel everything. I can-
not do this alone.

I'm not crying out here, I'm just being expressive. I need to
share with you my space because it's full of sorcery and words.
The feeling here rests in too much power to not think out
loud. This new invisible force of the world feels prophetic...yet
it keeps leaving a taste of a disturbia.

Nothing about this is close to insipience. This is more than a
once-a-month thing; this is a lifestyle thing...and I can't fuck-
ing do this alone.

My story

isn't the way

it is

just for me.

Disown

I'm pretty sure something foreign was on me. I could sense the intrusion. Even in my sleep it lingered. I couldn't find its source. I couldn't find its resting spot. Location unknown, purpose unknown.

So, I just breathed. I breathed it out in heated waves through every orifice of skin. I could feel it expelling from me as I tried to inhale what was next. I practiced and perfected the breaths; it became my craft. I breathed and I listened...and I listened and I breathed. I burned sage and candles, practiced visualization and drank ginger tea extra hot. I loved inside a little more deeply. I felt inside, a lot more deeply...remembering to inhale just as deep...whatever the intrusion was, whether it be doubt, or fear, denial or Covid-19...whatever it was, it's gone now.

For the Lineage

All the men that you encounter, will see you, they will feel your vibration and your light. But the way the universe of the goddesses is set up, not all men are designed to comprehend these riches. Most men won't be equipped to process your frequency. It's not a flaw in any design, it's a design incorporating protection for your excellency. Men whose internal entities can't fuck with yours will eventually never try. Your aura and your light will be so bright to other souls that your mere existence will be a natural filter.

Men of confidence, but truly not on your level will eventually fizzle out, for the better. There won't exist any space for them to rationalize what you could ever be to them; how powerful your presence could be, so that force, it stays away, awaiting its match.

When people are drawn to your light but they can't absorb it... it creates an almost hostile environment; the filtering will be your protection. Don't let it make you feel lonely, you have one thousand ancestors walking with you and working for your alignment. Only truth will step to you, only good intention, alignment and self-mastery will step to you.

Understand this power as a resource.

Respect it.

Honor it.

Fuel it.

Use it.

Wading in Water

I asked my spirit guide to help me, then I slept for 8 hours.

I heard him whisper that I was the most beautiful woman he had ever been close to, he wasn't close with his mother.

You know that feeling when your hands are freezing and you hold them under perfectly warm running water, that's how he feels.

I told him I don't have any more people to lose and I'd rather he not become one of them.

He changed the subject, he wanted to wade in the water...first just me, then, him with me.

He needed to watch me through the glassiest reflection, a liquid mirror, image distorted, from some sort of distance, moving the way the water wanted me.

Then to look upon me, face to face, with pristine attention, a comparison of some sort, visually captured in eyes made of glass, movement nonexistent for he needs to process this sight.

Sitting upon water that maybe existed, basking in feelings that used to reside in a buried space. He needed to feel the stillness, needed to feel the wholeness, needed desperately, to feel the completion.

He needed desperately to feel me from the inside, and that he did. He needed stringently to taste the light I would bring to fruition.

In this land where we wade in water that doesn't exist. The land where eyes pierce souls beyond ways described in literature. This land where enticement meets inviting. The woman sorrowfully alluring, passionately seductive, wading in water.

He told me it's the way my thighs connect to my hips. He insisted in its truth for he's applied great dedication studying the way I move, when he's at his closest. He insisted on this to be the origin of the magic he feeds on. I told him it comes from the root of me, not my pit, that it gets deeper than an energetic field, that it extends up my spine, existing as my entire being. That the alchemy only originates here permeating all stretches of my soul. I told him that I want to expel its entirety on him and with him forever.

He told me he knows.

He insisted that he always knew, ever since the first time we waded in water, that wasn't water.

The Human Comeback

I wanted to feel human. So, I sat with myself, until I began to sway, I moved to no particular beat. I moved until my joints pushed back. I moved in a full circle as I sat there, I experienced myself.

I sat there with myself. Because I wanted to feel human. If you sit still long enough, the body will tell you exactly what it needs.

February Sixteenth

Aliyah...

Today is your Birthday...it's also the day thirteen years ago, I was recreated to best serve you.

I became a mother to 'your highness'. I won't ever stray from that, even though the singleness of this parenting gets hard and society today scares me because even teenage goddesses are easily influenced.

This mothering...it's who I am in my soul and I love the way it feels. Literally, nothing else works for me. You have created purpose in me and I will always help create that for you. I advance myself continuously...it's the only way I can lead someone that's better than me. The divine in me, will always honor the divine in you.

With All of my Soul, All of my Love...Momsie.

Don't let your emotions or frustrations

rush through your life without

processing them. It will leave tire marks

and that's no one's aesthetic.

Writer Struggles

That moment you realize you want to write, but your thoughts are too basic.

Then you realize you'd rather make love, but your thoughts, they're too basic.

Am I Okay?

Do you know what that's like?

To not feel a person's care every day. For there to exist no voice...saying "it's going to be okay".

The moments when you want to hear those words so desperately, you don't even care if it's directed at you. Do you know what it feels like to be the most magical person you know...yet no one sees it?

Do you know how it feels to sit in a room full of laughing friends yet feel painfully alone?

Do you know how it feels to say goodbye to your parents forever; and to do everything in your power everyday hoping you'll never have to say goodbye to your daughter?

Do you know how hurtful separation anxiety can be because that daughter is all you have?

What does it mean when your hands are the only ones that touch you?

I know what these things feel like, so I know how to care, I know how to love and I'll always give it before I receive it.

Stop meeting beautiful men and wondering what they need from you.

Indo

There's a piece of matte black wall that I see when I'm with you. And I don't know if it represents calmness or chaos.

You don't resonate with me just like I don't resonate with you. You keep trying to hail Medusa but I'm not playing with you. I'll end up drinking from you, then we'll both be poisonous. You're trying to make this about my past but I just met you.

I think if the music was any louder, we'd hurt each other.

Writings on the Wall

I don't remember the day that it happened, but I do want you to hold my hand.

I want the skin to skin to feel like you're on the inside. I need the air in the room to taste like summer mornings in the 90s. I'm requiring the sound to be just that of the fingertips dragging across my skin. Have you ever heard that sound, it's lifeless, like your voice when you say you love me. A dry echo with persuasion at the least. I needed the twinkle in my eye to be understood more fully. I'd need those hand-held fans to never stop, and the psychedelics to make the writings on the wall come back.

Strings & Toils

So, you watched me manifest a bunch of shit.

But did you see me crying, on the middle of the Boulevard while I was stopped at a light that I thought was red?

Did you know that I toiled with the thought of...should I even do this, it's all happening too fast.

How about that yesterday, I stumbled, hard. I couldn't see through the stain glass stairs you suggested I take instead of the winding road.

And I think I found a stolen heart up there which almost broke mine. I need you to understand something, I get lost very easily, I'm not from around here, but even the tiniest string will help me remember.

Ramify

I gave him five months and then I gave him six. And he still doesn't love me. So, I sit with my love alone. I make sure it transcends to him when I trace the skin of his back. I make sure he can feel it through my pulsating flesh, saturated from all the crying out. Saturated from crying out in the pleasure of a lifetimes love gone awry. I make sure he feels it, every time. I make sure he hears it from my lips, in words that hold back of consisting of the word love. Indirectly fueling a fire that I hope will ramify into one too immense to continue to ignore. I tend to him like I need him. I touch his soul because that's how I want him. His voice is satisfying beyond ways of wording and the closeness, the closeness is, well... it's etched in time and it literally erases everything but us. Two bodies sharing one. That's what I've come back to because that's what I've been after. He doesn't know it, and I can never tell him because I gave him six months and then I gave him seven and he still doesn't love me.

Month Eight

I ran my fingers across his skin and I wondered if he loved me yet. It sure felt like he did as we lay there, I couldn't tell if I felt my heart beat inside me or his.

Our breathing may have been in sync, as we lay chest to chest but I couldn't tell because my head may have been in the clouds.

This closeness was what I wanted; these pauses in between sessions was exactly what I needed. The staying latched in, and it never coming out, I needed that more.

You see...my love language is touch, and his love language is sex and they say slow sex is just as good as a slow diet, so we're going to do both.

Fingers digging at the skin of his back while I bellow softly, to the rhythm of slow motion.

Because this slow sex, this barely sex, when you slow down just so you can feel it sex...that's when our souls communicate. And I know you know that I can hear you for you keep coming back to dump it all on me and in me. My love language is touch and his is sex, so this works.

Every night when we link for this link, he knows exactly how to convince me that love exists between us...after all he is my familiar, so I return the favor, but he still doesn't love me.

I know why he comes here, with his new mediocrity, so I make sure he feels superior. A superiority to anyone he might think is around, getting a dose of his dose.

He has no idea how deeply this belongs to him, I can't tell what's tainting him, I don't know if it's the drugs or the inferior women with whom he normally entangles.

He always shows up needing the full reup, the works, the top off always much heavier spiritually than it is sexually......or maybe it's a beautiful blend of both with a bold shot of repressed ego. I breathe life into this man literally, through my mouth and into his.

You see...A thousand years ago, I belonged to a king. And before that it was a god. And one of the times, it might have been him.

And he still kind of feels like royalty sometimes, even magic but it's not from this life, no, clearly, he's been downgraded. It's from a different life where we were better...and now he's a liar, falsely identifying himself and that's deeply triggering! I told him I'd follow his lead at the beginning of our story and I meant it like I do this poem.

He always comes having half of the story, he presents himself on his knees, half understanding the energies at work and why him. He comes needing to feel like the one that satisfies unfaltering...the man that's my favorite. So repetitively, time after time, I give him that, with loving caresses that speak volumes about his intimacy. The same intimacy he wants me to think is personalized for me...but I know it's practiced with everyone now. So, I keep practicing too with the kisses, and the hands he calls magic, with the caresses and the echoes, with the screaming of his name and the whispering of his name.

I see into him when he plugs into me and it feels toxic but its sexiness is something I need. Clearly, he's been demoted over the centuries with this spiritual decline, but I still love him, that's the arrangement between souls. And there's something about the way he doesn't use his tongue or his words that triggers the villain in me and if that's triggering, then you can call me a gypsy or a sorcerer, or a healer, or an enchantress, or an oracle or a god, whatever makes this less alarming...just don't say I'm unknowing, because before all these things my power is that I am a woman.

Misconstrued

It feels warm, like too warm, like an oven that gets too hot, like a Sinister battle between two evils, both Goddesses. It travels through parts that bear way more magic than before. This was supposed to be a black out, but sometimes I'm imperial without trying, sometimes I can feel the retrograde in my chest, sometimes things become flagitious...without trying. Sometimes the ever-watchful eyes need to happen, mesmerized by the effortless nobility, and the not so by accident lascivious undertone...noticing the hieroglyphs adorning her skin in increments, that dote passive aggression...images painted incorrectly for they have no disclosure. Demand is high, supply, to be determined. It's not just the nighttime that I feel this way, I think too many people are dreaming about me.

Everything Beautiful

"It's everything beautiful".

I whispered, in a search for air, although relaxation was amidst.

I can feel it heavy right here. I touched my chest, lying on my back, fingers resting gracefully while my chest rose and fell. His hand crept on top of mine while his body followed. Thighs automatic because I can always taste his air before his lips touch me. I love him. He moves at the speed of time. He knows that there is no time. I feel the vibration begin to climb, it lives in my skin, he lives in my skin, weighted. His weight on me, this weight of his spirit, I give in to it. This man is divine. He is grace. He is truth. I have to keep this.

"This feels like everything beautiful", it escapes my lips, only for me to hear, though my lips brush against his face. I love him. This man is my gentle friend, he leaves no voids without trying. This is a privilege, in all caps. I mean, where is this place? How did we get here please and thank you. We can just keep floating here in this realm where time is not of the essence, in the clouds, without the sky. Where I whisper to him without enough air, "this feels like everything beautiful".

Beneath the King

I didn't walk this way on purpose, this is what I was given. I didn't take heed to the message, there actually was no choosing. There was no line up of astrology to vacillate, this was placed on me. This aura isn't rich in essence, encased in chemistry due to my placing, nor to his ranking, this was thrown on me. There was no, do I or don't I.

I was thrown at the feet of what I thought was a wizard.

So, I did what I do best.

Banished

Dreams and aspirations can shatter...just like my feelings did.

If the air was too thick, you shouldn't have spoke my name.

If the sounds too cerebral...you shouldn't have listened with your face in between my legs. If you didn't want to be up here with me you should have settled for acrophobia when I tried to banish you. If you didn't want to coordinate up from down, we shouldn't have sung those hymns together, and I'm not an alto...I'm a soprano. If you didn't want my uncovered skin in the grass, you shouldn't have put that flower in my hair.

If you didn't love this, you shouldn't have swallowed. And if you were never going to feel meaningful, your opening statement should have been a lie.

I'm not a killer...but don't push me...that's how the saying goes right?!

Are women of magic allowed to say that?

Our First Hug

Blurred curls pulsate to a rhythmic heart. Lashes touch in slow motion. A feeling of sitting still yet moving too fast. I barely breathe because if I do...you'd vanish. I haven't had this dream yet, I've never been present for this speed. I knew it wasn't true, I knew you weren't gone. There's no sense that would have made, for you to be gone in an instant a week before your daughter starts senior year. I knew you weren't gone. Breathing slowly, I ponder rising to my feet, at just the thought of it the clouds disappeared ejecting me from my seat. And there you stood, just as I remembered you. I needed to touch you just one more time. And there's always been that hug I never got. I can do that now. A displaced fear no longer exists.

I wasn't able to give you that as a child girl whose trust in men had been stolen but I can now, I'm here now.

I'm here in this space with you now! You allowed me to come see you because I'm healed right? I can touch your hand now and feel the power of you. I can touch your hand now and feel the strength of what a father's love can do.

I can hold onto you, my shoulders resting with yours, heart chakra to heart chakra, the bridge of my nose pressed closely against your neck, my hands locked around your back, with no fear, only love, with no regrets, only appreciation, with no hesitation, only respect. I didn't need any words, you were in my mind, you heard the thoughts and I hugged you tighter, I miss you so much. In this chance to breathe you in, you spoke to me in clear concise words, words of power as my eyes melted from the inside...

"The sacrifice I made will be worth it every time, you can settle down now, your loss is done. Any of the people you appoint are protected, we are granting you that. Your only concern is staying true to your mission, change this world."

When you find someone that will

respect you even in your absence.

Never let them go. And return the

favor.

Howl at the Moon

If I whispered your name while I was with another, nestled against his face, in the deep hours of the night, would you hear it?

If I told you it was still you, would you believe me? Remember that time I told you I'd do anything you want if you howl at the moon with me? This is that.

Have you ever had an abstract dream, of which you couldn't find words...or pictures.

That's how this feels.

It feels the way you used to, meticulous but unclear. Lucid, but, with all your perimeters.

You feel the way wading in water does. Unnecessary....but necessary.

Shadowing

Do you want to lovingly remove the earth from my shoulders and sit with me in the grass while we sort of bask in the sun? Sort of because most of our skin will be covered in one another's skin that basking will become shadowing. Let us tell some tales about what we want out of life. Let us spill some secrets about how much of life we are willing to take. Don't be deceptive, you've known from the moment that I summoned you that I could undoubtedly see right through you.

Fairy God Mother

I need someone to need me beyond anything reasonable. And you're the only one that I touch so that's going to be you. I have sleepless nights pondering without planning, how to make you crazy. I'll scribble in that worn out diary, "why the fuck doesn't he love me yet?!" You see, to a human woman, this is what being in love would feel like, but for me...actually...let me introduce myself.

I'm stubborn to nothing imaginable, I have a sexual insatiably that's down right unfair. I need you and you and you and you and you to always, face first, eyes right here, watch me perform, even when I'm not. Minds envisioning an undressing in slow motion then reversed, I mean, this dress that slips down to even thicker thighs than you imagined, then doesn't... boomerang!

Wet hair dripping on already enough beads on oily skin, fingers crawling from hair to parted lips, across my chest, to a waist that's had plenty of kisses but needs more...droplets of water cascading through waistlines and around hips, I'd need you to drink of this, and chase it with whatever I want. You can't fight it, you need this, this is an enchantment. In this storm, I thunder.

Signed,
Your fairy, your god, your mother.

This Oracle, If You Will

She felt to me like a wounded bird, I thought this silently as I plucked another feather. She was so beautiful, even the tiny eyes beaded in black were mesmerizing. Placing hands upon her chest, felt like such a thing I could never achieve on my own. An energy absorbed into mine, a meter now full...her, left with the crawl, as I yet again, plucked another feather.

She twists and turns, unsure if my intention is loving or menacing. "It's loving", I say just to myself, as my plan of ending her soaring comes closer to fruition. And so, I told her I loved her but I didn't say it, the touch of my hands against the softest feathers feed that lie better than my deceitful tongue ever could.

Once upon a time, she told me that once upon a time, someone told her that men can be jealous of powerful women, I laughed silently as I plucked her final feather.

Or So You Thought

I brushed my fingers gently across his lips and thought of ending him. Instead, I kissed him between his brows, he felt none of it. And so, I left him there in his slumber, on his final high, his clip emptied, the fantasies fulfilled. Surrounded by his plants, all named after my names. Surrounded by his paintings that will all be replaced by amateur hand paintings of me, full of curls and silhouette, the most craved. In his space once complete, gradually feeling less complete as the mishandled gifts return home.

Do you know what he will be wishing in a few days' time? That he never toyed with the plucking of feathers that always grow back...

The goddesses body produces an

unlimited amount of tears just like it

does cum, I'm not willing to do both

for you.

Dear John

Tears were all over my back because I wanted to sleep naked and compiling that dear John text to you ran longer than I anticipated.

I wanted to feel something different. I started off in another realm, another mode, perhaps even another dimension. I wanted my hair to brush against the skin of your face after I piled myself gingerly into your lap.

I wanted there to be much more breathing than talking this time. I wanted you to listen harder this time, than ever before, I wanted the sky to witness our closeness. I wanted the moon to direct the stars of when to tune in more fully. I wanted there to be kisses this time. I wanted to be painted by the tips of your fingers and the entire body of your tongue. I wanted you to let me finish my sentence. I wanted you to let me finish my climax. I wanted you to face me this time. I wanted you to look at me so I could finally see you. I wanted you to pull my head back by the roots of my hair, licking me from my neck to my lips and for you to tell me you loved me. I wanted you to make actual love to me, invasive and slow...like you promised.

Then confirmation came and the stomach pain was back and so was I and the smell of your beard in my bedsheets reminded me that this was over.

I could remember back to the time when I thought, all we need is more and we are sure to find love. But that never happened. At one point I thought that I loved you, and at another point I was sure you were him and at the last point I realized you were convenient. And sometimes, sometimes but not lately you were good for my ego, you know, the version of me I don't even want to know. So this is my goodbye, this is that dear John letter that's just for me. And you, you will get ghosted and if you suffer from the needing closure illusion you can consult the sacred text, "OSYT".

If a quality that you love about a person is teachable, is it even really that special?

An Experience

I don't want to just have sex; I want to have an experience. I'd love to know that this brings you alive as much as it does me. We won't make love because this will already be love. When you kiss my collarbone, I want it to be because you love the way my skin breathes, and you can't not smell me. The tiny hairs that perch my skin, you need to visit them, you love them. The marks of beauty sprinkled softly over the collar bone and throat; you're convinced they excrete essential oils. You like the way my lips rest between yours, in between kisses. And the way my mouth never closes. You say, my skin was designed for your touch and the double hip cleavage was designed for your tongue. Pheromones, the fragrance you follow meticulously from the center of untamed curls to French painted toes, you tell me you would bottle me. You say love spell lotion is a joke and that this is a hypnotism. A hypnotism you'll always allow, a center piece, never arm candy. You take me into you understanding this love is the greatest space. I take you into me cradling in the warmth of your skin, nothing hollow this time, unshaken at the thought that this is the experience we're going to use to create life and more love.

Meet the Team

I'm not in control of my feelings for the other souls; my spirit guides deal with that.

Here, since you like to look at lines and shapes and specimens of men, here, he will show you what heartbreak feels like for the human, this will build character, this will mark the beginning of your legacy. He will give you "Her" and you will see what your rivals are truly like. The apology for why you had to endure so long will be the gift of forgiveness...he will be a forgotten love and your tears will begin to feel warmer, more controlled.

And this one here, he is practice. He will level you up for the ones that line up in 2020. Feel the difference here between tapping into reception versus tapping into none. He is practice because at some point you needed to understand that the darkness was always us, never step foot over here, your shine is more than gold. If they crumble or fall it was always us. There was no need to make that call, he would have never hurt you, we made it physically impossible. You will exit here easier than the others, the Sirens will be waiting. Tears growing warmer, more deliberate.

This one will be heavier than practice, this is an apprentice-ship, this electricity is what you've been preparing for...use it as you wish, but do no harm. If he wants you to stay, stay with him...once upon a time you were his queen...once upon another time, you were the servant he valued more than his queen. He will have a final chance at reunion, in which he will fail, the ego gets him every time. Remain close enough to evoke persuasion, you are his spirit guide.

But moving on...remove your shades when you see "Him", don't lower them, take them off. Remove your veil and your dress. He's going to look through you and grant all access, yes all of it. He is the one you laid with in the beginning, the one that shared his voice before you had yours, he is the one who gives us communication, he is the one that keeps us together, even when you suggest side questing. He will come with one kiss, that's all you will need. Touch his hands the way you touch your heart chakra. Don't kiss his body, he finds that offensive. Instead, show him that your walk with high pos-ture makes sense now, lay with him, returning that favor, share with him your voice, show what your vibrational pull can do, share your growth...so he knows it was all for a reason, so he knows mission complete.

Or Whatever Your Name Is

Dear.......Covid,

Or whatever your name is.

I believe in my healing capabilities. I'm not so sure about you. You're the first identifiable thing that tried to threaten my safety shield, and you tried to scare my daughter. But that didn't work, we only laughed at you because we play survival games for a living. We turned you into a 90's "Zombie Apocalypse" game that we beat on the hardest level, twice.

And let me tell you a little bit about what you didn't change. You didn't change anyone's idea about what it takes to live a good life, you didn't change any one's concept of what it means to practice good karma either. And you also didn't change anything at all regarding the spiritual collective, you haven't slowed us down.

And you damn sure didn't change my daughter's perception of a good zombie apocalypse game, we're looking forward to a sequel.

The universe is still keeping me very much organically charged, so I'm still download ready, and I continue to have just enough collective complaints that I can manifest blanket solutions for all, giving me just enough appreciators to feel charged even on a waning moon. And to be honest, you're not important enough to stay on topic, and this is a rough draft and this was actually a burn after writing thing.

Anyway, fuck you.

Dear People,

I started writing poetry eight years ago and I write the most NOT when my fear is high but when my emotions are high... people...you do that for me. Nothing will EVER change that.

People, thank you.

A Closer Look

But if you look a little closer, unplanned crevices and cracks you will see, they're not etched out by man, only time, eons and eons of time. Fine lines to represent the process and the progress...and if you look even closer...these smile lines, they're the work of some being not keen in symmetry. There's gold and pixels of crystals here...that the high light naturally highlights.

And the men, you do continue to catch my eye, but blinders and filters reject these representatives...then there's the empath in me that tries to correct the incorrect, trying to exchange healing for love, but one can't save the person not aware of their sinking...and one cannot bless the ones unworthy. And outside the perimeter, you can imagine all the lace, not on me like you prefer but inside with the rest of the magic, the antiquity; while the ancestral lineage plays hymns, orchestrating lexicons, on sidelines governed by the Father of Wizards. Backstreets and all paths in and around protected by governing parties. I love that you love all of this but I need more. Unable to fall into love, I continue to create, working with a soul whose language I can finally understand. A soul of whose alignment I have unequivocally mastered. Manifesting and speaking this into existence. I'm doing the work and I will forever, with stringent sending's of both love and light, the amplification of people pleasing. Meanwhile I will stay perched up high, banished, out of reach, waiting until...both she...and he.

Casting Beautiful Nets

For so long, I felt like all I was supposed to be was a mom. There was so much safety in that for me.

Then I sat the down, slowed down, close to removed from the programming.

And then I met you, while I was pretty solid. And I thought about loving a stranger. I thought about connecting with an energy in an extension beyond mothering. I thought about the friendliness of you and I thought...maybe my casting of that beautiful net FINALLY worked. I thought maybe, maybe I caught something beautiful.

And then I thought, have I earned this? Do I deserve this? And I tried to think of manifestation and the beauty of you and my beautiful net...

But instead, I thought of death again and loss again and abandonment again. I thought about how I always wonder, what's the point, love always leaves. I thought about how people have walked away from me more often than they've stayed and I thought of the burn from that. The burn that you can remember because it lives on the skin of the entire chest, able to be recalled at a moment's notice. And then I felt the burn, in

THAT moment's notice, alongside fear, and the thought, do I deserve this.

And then, you touched my hand...and I thought of you and how beautiful you were...and the idea that this might be my life now. And that I think you may have kissed all the parts of my skin that the sensation of burning pain lives. I thought of you. And I thought of your hand and I thought...maybe I can be a mother, and the friend that's beyond a friend. I thought, I can safely and securely love this man, because he is my friend, he's going to help me weave a more beautiful, larger net. It will finally be the casting of the beautiful net I've always worked toward...all the sacrifice worth it.

My Poetry at Last

And then I whispered; my lips resting gently with his, cool heated breath exchanged in waves, his hands never stopped being in my hair, his pelvis never rising from mine, the transparency almost felt wrong, the heaviness of an eye gaze made of a love requiring no words felt more dangerous than before, I found a perfect space in between the softest breathing lips, I kissed him with a kiss whose intention was forever...

"it's always been you that I wrote of...you feel like poetry"

And I wondered,

"Does this make me a witch?"

About the Author

Nicole Jennifer Milburn is a native of Philadelphia Pennsylvania, currently residing in South Jersey. She is a Reiki master, a practitioner of spirituality and holistic health, and has a love for all things natural. Nicole is a firm believer that everyone should look to and embrace the ingrained source of energy within. Nicole mindfully embraces the divine feminine energy within her and expresses that passionately through her work as a Birth Doula and Cosmic Sexuality instructor.

Nicole grew up in Northeast Philadelphia where she was raised by her father, who was also a writer. Her father introduced her to poetry writing at a young age, however, it didn't resonate until much later in her life. Twenty years later, driven by her love of being a mother, Nicole wrote her first poem. Being able to express ideas and thoughts through poetry allows Nicole to feel close to her father who passed away in 2002.

Nicole's interest in writing poetry extends beyond her bond with her father and her love for the journey of motherhood. It also creates a space for her to share experiences and feelings that can be relatable and empowering to all women.

"Writing poetry feels like a very safe space for my curiosity and creativity. Our curiosity and creativity should always be in motion, it's one of the best things we can do for ourselves on our never-ending journey of growth."

Nicole Jennifer Milburn
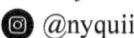 @nyquii

www.ingramcontent.com/pod-product-compliance
Lightning Source LLC
Chambersburg PA
CBHW030015070526
44668CB00015B/908